D1423084

MAL

ROTHERHAM LIBRARY & INFORMATION SERVICE

This book must be returned by the date specified at the time of issue as
the DUE DATE FOR RETURN
The loan may be extended (personally, by post, telephone or online) for
a further period, if the book is not required by another reader, by quoting
the barcode / author / title.

Enquiries: 01709 336774

www.rotherham.gov.uk/libraries

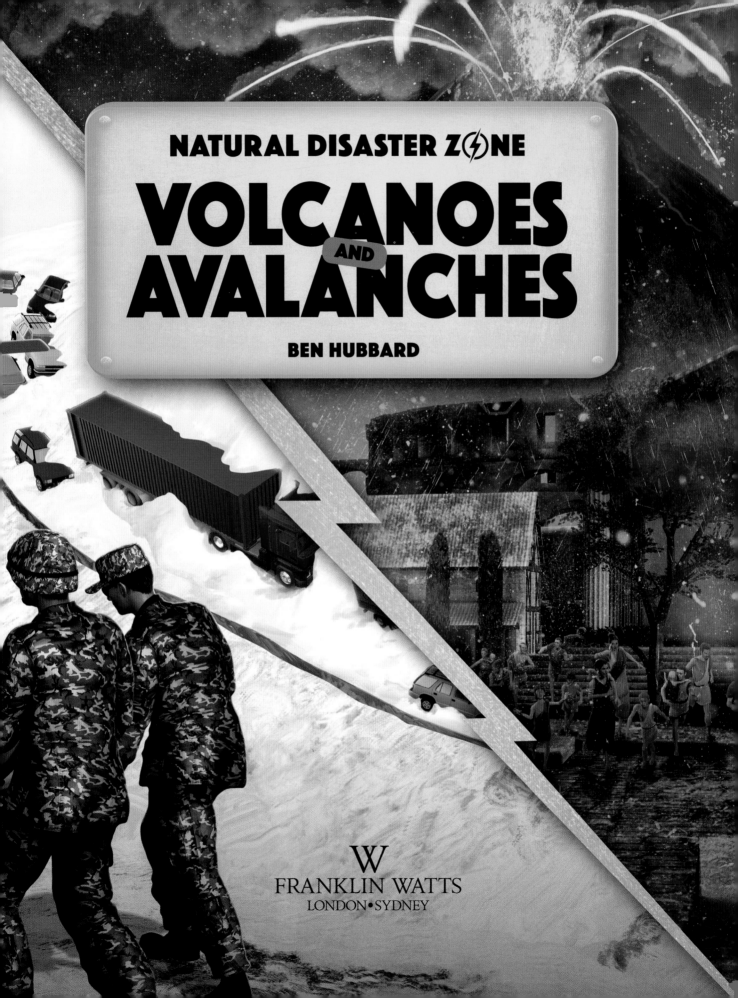

NATURAL DISASTER Z⚡NE
VOLCANOES AND AVALANCHES

BEN HUBBARD

W
FRANKLIN WATTS
LONDON • SYDNEY

Franklin Watts
First published in Great Britain in 2019 by The Watts Publishing Group

Copyright © The Watts Publishing Group, 2019

All rights reserved.

Credits
Editor: Elise Short
Illustration and Design: Collaborate Agency

Picture credits:
All additional images courtesy of Shutterstock.

Every attempt has been made to clear copyright. Should there be any inadvertent
omission please apply to the publisher for rectification.

HB ISBN 978 1 4451 6573 8
PB ISBN 978 1 4451 6574 5

Printed in China

MIX
Paper from
responsible sources
FSC® C104740

Franklin Watts
An imprint of
Hachette Children's Group
Part of The Watts Publishing Group
Carmelite House
50 Victoria Embankment
London EC4Y 0DZ

An Hachette UK Company
www.hachette.co.uk

www.franklinwatts.co.uk

Rotherham Libraries	
B55 048 659 7	
PETERS	20-Aug-2019
J551.21	£12.99
	MAL

CONTENTS

Introducing Volcanoes and Avalanches 4

When a Volcano Erupts 6

What's in a Volcano? 8

Types of Volcanoes 10

Rock, Gas, Ash and Lava 12

CASE STUDY: Vesuvius, CE 79 14

Supervolcanoes 16

People and Volcanoes 18

When an Avalanche is Released 20

What's in an Avalanche? 22

Avalanche Types 24

People and Avalanches 26

CASE STUDY: Huascaran, 1970 28

Glossary, Books and Helpful Websites 30

Index 32

Introducing Volcanoes and Avalanches

Volcanoes and avalanches are among the most violent and devastating natural disasters on Earth. Both are sudden, extreme and difficult to predict. When they strike, volcanoes and avalanches inflict very different forms of destruction on the people and buildings around them. So what are these natural disasters?

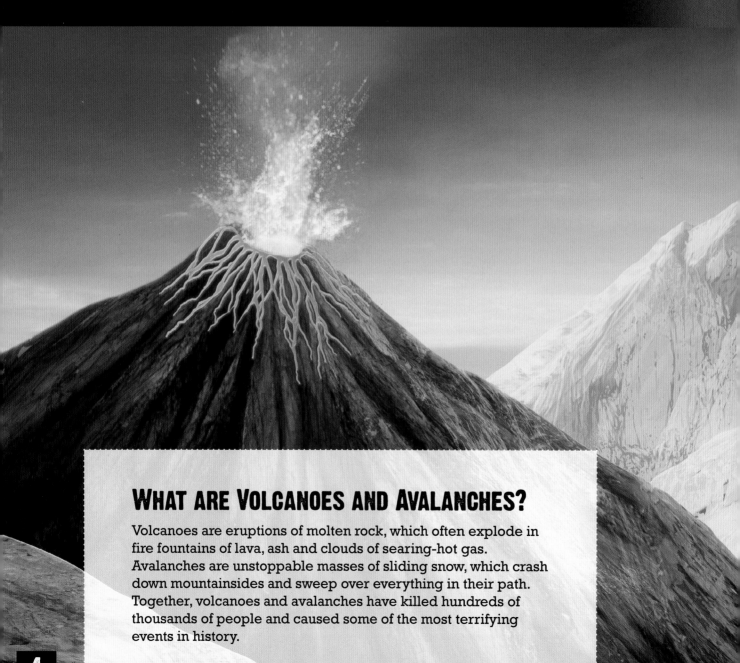

What are Volcanoes and Avalanches?

Volcanoes are eruptions of molten rock, which often explode in fire fountains of lava, ash and clouds of searing-hot gas. Avalanches are unstoppable masses of sliding snow, which crash down mountainsides and sweep over everything in their path. Together, volcanoes and avalanches have killed hundreds of thousands of people and caused some of the most terrifying events in history.

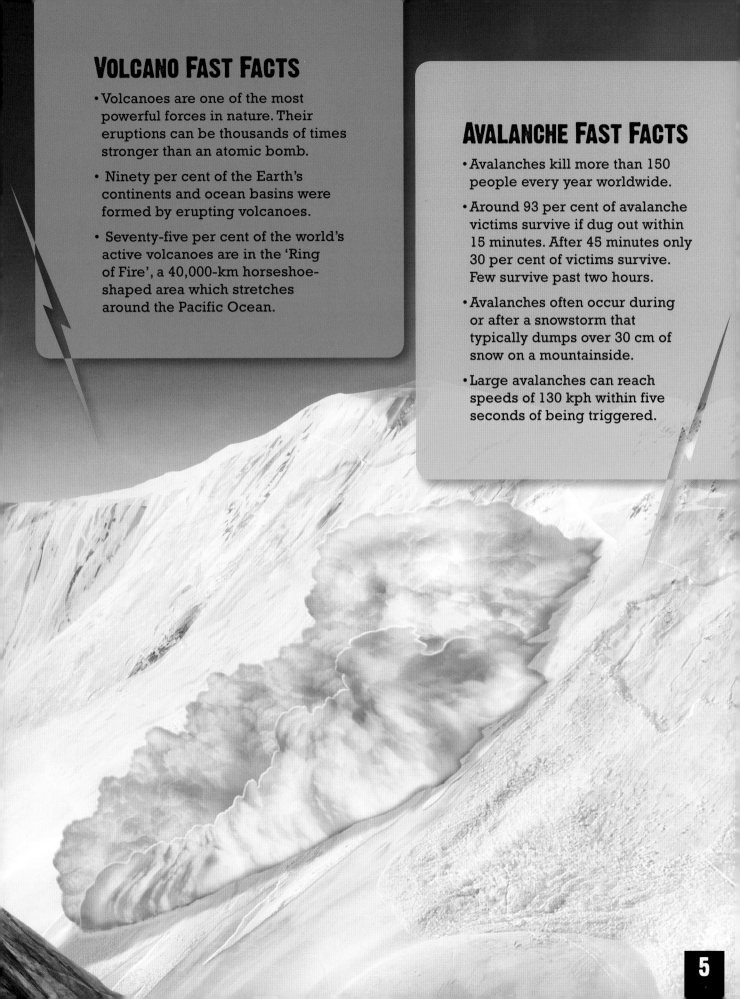

VOLCANO FAST FACTS

- Volcanoes are one of the most powerful forces in nature. Their eruptions can be thousands of times stronger than an atomic bomb.

- Ninety per cent of the Earth's continents and ocean basins were formed by erupting volcanoes.

- Seventy-five per cent of the world's active volcanoes are in the 'Ring of Fire', a 40,000-km horseshoe-shaped area which stretches around the Pacific Ocean.

AVALANCHE FAST FACTS

- Avalanches kill more than 150 people every year worldwide.

- Around 93 per cent of avalanche victims survive if dug out within 15 minutes. After 45 minutes only 30 per cent of victims survive. Few survive past two hours.

- Avalanches often occur during or after a snowstorm that typically dumps over 30 cm of snow on a mountainside.

- Large avalanches can reach speeds of 130 kph within five seconds of being triggered.

WHEN A VOLCANO ERUPTS

In September 2010, small earthquakes were reported on Mount Merapi, a volcano on the Island of Java in Indonesia. On 23 October, lava began flowing from the volcano. With an eruption imminent, villagers within a 10-km radius were ordered to evacuate. Merapi was about to begin its deadliest eruption in over 100 years.

INDIA

INDONESIA

Mount Merapi

FIREBALLS AND GAS

On 25 October, Merapi began a series of explosive eruptions that blasted fireballs, ash and lava 6 km into the air. The volcano also sent a searing 800°C cloud of gas down its densely-populated slopes. As it reached speeds of 100 kph, this cloud, called a pyroclastic flow, burnt trees, homes and locals trying to escape. It then blanketed villages 15 km away in 20 cm of ash.

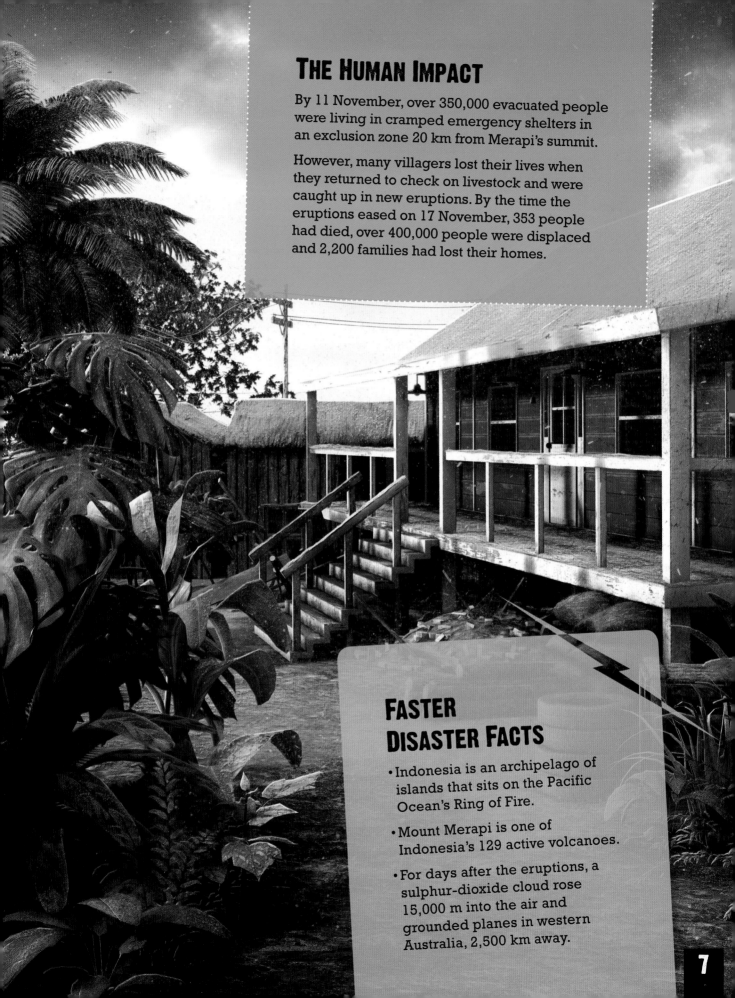

THE HUMAN IMPACT

By 11 November, over 350,000 evacuated people were living in cramped emergency shelters in an exclusion zone 20 km from Merapi's summit.

However, many villagers lost their lives when they returned to check on livestock and were caught up in new eruptions. By the time the eruptions eased on 17 November, 353 people had died, over 400,000 people were displaced and 2,200 families had lost their homes.

FASTER DISASTER FACTS

- Indonesia is an archipelago of islands that sits on the Pacific Ocean's Ring of Fire.

- Mount Merapi is one of Indonesia's 129 active volcanoes.

- For days after the eruptions, a sulphur-dioxide cloud rose 15,000 m into the air and grounded planes in western Australia, 2,500 km away.

WHAT'S IN A VOLCANO?

A volcano is formed when red-hot, molten rock called magma bursts through a weak spot in the Earth's surface. Once it reaches the surface this magma is called lava. Lava can ooze out slowly or be flung violently into the sky alongside ash, rock and deadly gases.

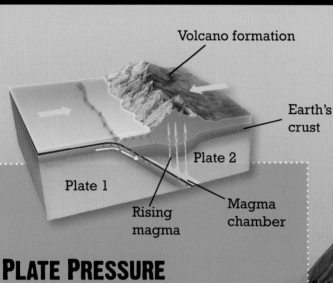

Volcano formation

Earth's crust

Plate 2

Plate 1

Rising magma

Magma chamber

PLATE PRESSURE

Magma sits in large wells called magma chambers, which lie deep beneath the Earth's crust. The crust is formed of vast slabs of rock called tectonic plates, which are constantly moving.

When one plate moves over another, it pushes it down into the Earth's mantle. This causes some of the sinking plate's rock to melt into magma, which then rises to form a volcano. Volcanoes can also form in the gap where two plates move apart.

Magma from the magma chamber feeds into a volcano's main vent.

Magma lies in a chamber below the volcano where it is under great pressure.

Lava fountains and fireballs can erupt from a volcano's crater and a cloud of ash and gases can be sent 30 km high into the air.

The volcano is formed from cooled layers of lava, rock and ash.

Fissures called secondary vents can break off from the main vent and cause secondary cones.

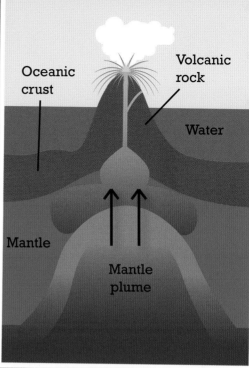

Oceanic crust

Volcanic rock

Water

Mantle

Mantle plume

HOT SPOTS

The largest volcanoes are formed by abnormally hot magma inside the Earth's mantle. Regions where this occurs are known as hot spots. The magma rises to the surface in mantle plumes and punches a hole through the tectonic plate to create a volcano. A hot spot created Hawaii's Mauna Loa, which is the world's second largest volcano.

Types of Volcanoes

Volcanoes come in a variety of shapes and sizes: from simple cracks in the ground to majestic, cone-shaped mountains. A volcano's particular type is determined by the magma that feeds it. There are four main types of volcano: shield volcanoes, stratovolcanoes, cinder cones and lava domes.

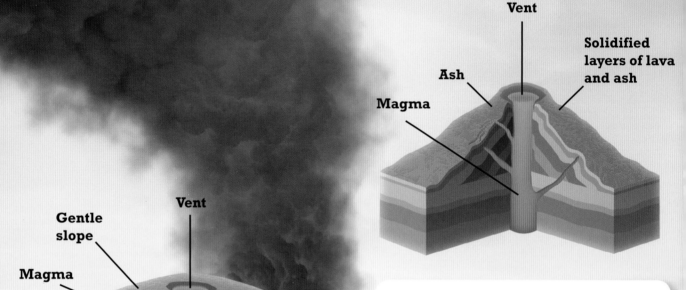

Shield Volcano

Low and bowl-shaped, a shield volcano is formed from thin, runny lava, which flows down its gentle slopes and cools slowly. Because the lava is thin, it allows plenty of gas to escape with it. This prevents an explosive eruption.

Stratovolcanoes

Built up from many layers of ash, rock and sticky lava, stratovolcanoes, also called composite volcanoes, are formed by explosive eruptions. The eruptions occur when sticky lava prevents gas from escaping and causes pressure to build up. Over time, the erupted lava forms a cone shape.

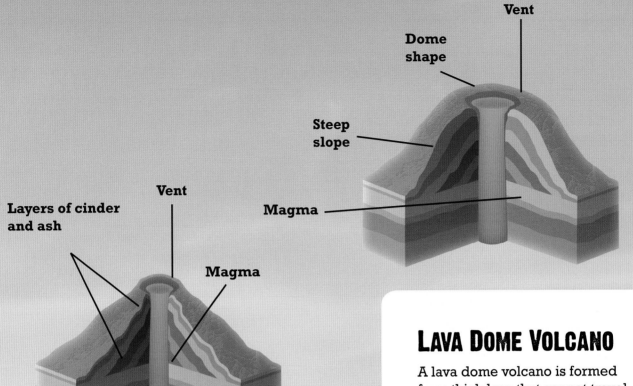

Vent

Dome shape

Steep slope

Magma

Layers of cinder and ash

Vent

Magma

LAVA DOME VOLCANO

A lava dome volcano is formed from thick lava that cannot travel far and simply piles up around its main vent. Hardened lava sometimes blocks the vent, leading to an explosion that blows off its top.

CINDER CONE VOLCANO

Cinder cone volcanoes are circular or oval-shaped and are formed from small pieces of lava and ash that blast into the air and cool after they reach the ground. The ash and lava then form layers around the top of the volcano's vent.

ACTIVE, DORMANT, EXTINCT

Volcanoes are described as being active, dormant or extinct. If a volcano is active, it erupts frequently. If it is classified as dormant, a volcano hasn't erupted in the past 10,000 years but is expected to erupt again. Extinct volcanoes are not expected to ever erupt again.

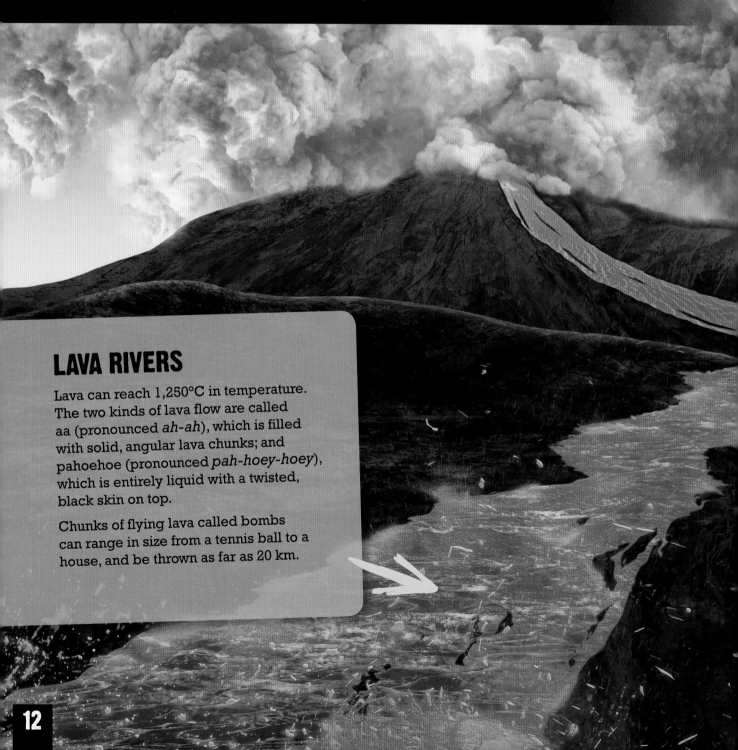

ROCK, GAS, ASH AND LAVA

The most explosive volcano eruptions spew out rivers of lava, hurl 'bombs' into the air, and release vast clouds of ash and toxic gases into the sky. Most deadly of all are the pyroclastic flows that rush down a volcano's slopes. Combined, these volcanic events can bring widespread destruction and a great loss of human life.

LAVA RIVERS

Lava can reach 1,250°C in temperature. The two kinds of lava flow are called aa (pronounced *ah-ah*), which is filled with solid, angular lava chunks; and pahoehoe (pronounced *pah-hoey-hoey*), which is entirely liquid with a twisted, black skin on top.

Chunks of flying lava called bombs can range in size from a tennis ball to a house, and be thrown as far as 20 km.

POISONOUS GAS

Dangerous gases released during an eruption can destroy crops and suffocate animals and humans. There are four main types of volcanic gas.

Sulphur dioxide and hydrogen chloride are acidic gases that can burn people's eyes and eat through their clothes, while carbon dioxide is an odourless killer that is difficult to detect.

Clouds of sulphur dioxide and carbon dioxide trapped in the atmosphere can block the Sun and cause acid rain. Water vapour is another gas released by volcanic eruptions.

PYROCLASTIC FLOWS

A pyroclastic flow is a fast-moving current of hot gas and volcanic matter that can move at 160 kph, reach temperatures of 800 °C, and flatten and incinerate everything in its path. Large pyroclastic flows spread like a blanket across hundreds of square kilometres and can leave whole settlements buried.

LAHARS

A lahar is a fast-moving mixture of pyroclastic debris, mud and water that can wash away whole villages. In 1985, over 23,000 people were killed when Colombia's Nevado del Ruiz volcano erupted. This caused four lahars which travelled at 50 kph to wash away the town of Armero at the foot of the volcano.

CASE STUDY: VESUVIUS, CE 79

History's most famous volcanic eruption took place in CE 79 near Naples in Italy. Here, Mount Vesuvius erupted over the Roman towns of Pompeii and Herculaneum, catching the local inhabitants completely unawares. Panic, deadly pyroclastic flows and the extraordinary preservation of the towns followed.

FRANCE

ITALY

Mount Vesuvius

ERUPTION

Vesuvius erupted at midday on 24 August. Pumice, hot ash and rock rained down on Pompeii and Herculaneum and turned the sky black as they blocked out the Sun.

At midnight, a series of deadly pyroclastic flows surged down the volcano's slopes and engulfed the towns. The searing heat and suffocating gas killed over 2,000 people almost instantly. The towns were then buried under 7 m of volcanic debris.

- The preserved towns of Pompeii and Herculaneum provided a snapshot in time from the Roman civilisation. Historians discovered many Roman artefacts and learned much about Roman life.

- The CE 79 eruptions were not Mount Vesuvius's first. In 1800 BCE, another eruption wiped out local Bronze Age settlements.

- Today, volcanologists predict Vesuvius will erupt again sometime in the future.

AFTERMATH

After the eruptions, the towns of Pompeii and Herculaneum stayed buried until the 18th century. Then, archaeologists began excavating the undisturbed sites.

The bodies of the dead had long since disappeared with time, leaving hollow 3D imprints in the solid volcanic debris. Archaeologists filled these imprints with plaster before digging them out.

SUPERVOLCANOES

Supervolcanoes are Earth's largest and most powerful volcanoes. An erupting supervolcano produces over 1,000 times more lava than a normal volcano. It can have a devastating impact on the Earth's ecology. However, no human has ever seen a supervolcano erupt. The last eruption took place 26,500 years ago.

YELLOWSTONE GIANT

The most famous of the world's 20 supervolcanoes is in Yellowstone National Park, USA. Today, Yellowstone's 56 km by 80 km caldera is a popular tourist attraction filled with colourful geysers and hot-water springs.

But 640,000 years ago, Yellowstone erupted with enough force to blast 1,000 cubic km of lava, dust and ash into the atmosphere. That is enough debris to bury a city to a depth of several kilometres.

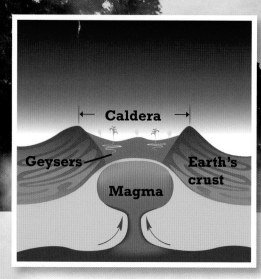

EXPLOSIVE ERUPTION

Built over hot spots in the Earth's mantle, supervolcanoes usually erupt with such explosive power that the ground collapses and only a shallow crater called a caldera is left.

Deep below the caldera is a vast magma chamber with molten rock that is under intense pressure. When an eruption is imminent, this pressure becomes like trying to keep a football under water. In the end, the magma has no place to go but up.

PREDICT NOT PREVENT

Scientists monitor Yellowstone carefully for signs of seismic activity. They hope there will be enough time to predict a future eruption, because no one will be able to prevent it.

A Yellowstone eruption could cover the surrounding 800 km in 10 cm of ash and send an umbrella cloud of gases into the atmosphere that could block out the Sun. This could cause severe climate change that would result in widespread crop failure and famine.

PEOPLE AND VOLCANOES

Expert scientists who travel around the world to study erupting volcanoes are called volcanologists. They do hot, dangerous work which involves getting closer to one of nature's most destructive forces than many would dare. By predicting when a volcano is about to erupt, volcanologists are responsible for saving the lives of those who live nearby.

TOOLS OF THE TRADE

Volcanologists rely on several tools to take samples from red-hot lava flows, monitor the poisonous gases escaping from the volcano's vent, measure tremors in the Earth, and stay safe.

NOTEBOOK

When a volcanologist arrives at a volcano, the first thing they do is make a full survey of the area. This involves drawing sketches and taking notes in a notebook. Laptops and digital cameras are also used. A special glass bottle on a pole is sometimes used to collect gas samples.

SAFETY SUIT

A proximity suit is a full-body, heat-shield suit that allows volcanologists to get close to a lava flow or the rim of an active volcano. The suit ensures no area is exposed to lava flows, which can burn and blister skin. Heat-proof boots also enable scientists to withstand extreme temperatures underfoot.

VOLCANO MONITORING

Volcano observatories have been built around the world to monitor local volcanoes. They provide updates based on new seismic activity and changes in gases expelled by volcanoes. Founded in 1814, the Vesuvius Observatory is the oldest volcano observatory in the world.

SEISMOMETER

Instruments that measure seismic activity, called seismometers, are one of a volcanologist's main tools for predicting eruptions. These are placed on, or in, the ground where they send signals via a satellite Internet connection. Tremors in the earth around a volcano often precede an eruption.

ROCK HAMMER

A volcanologist's most essential tool is a small rock hammer. This is used to chip off samples of rock and lava and collect them for analysis in a laboratory. Learning what rocks are made of and how they were formed is one of a volcanologist's main tasks.

WHEN AN AVALANCHE IS RELEASED

On 9 February 2010, a freak storm struck the Hindu Kush mountainside above the Salang Pass, Afghanistan. Torrential rain and ferocious winds loosened the mountain snow and set off a series of avalanches that trapped motorists along the road and tunnel below. It became a race against time to dig the motorists out.

Salang
Pass

AFGHANISTAN

PAKISTAN

INDIA

BRING IN THE ARMY

Afghan National Army helicopters were rushed to the avalanche site alongside 500 soldiers armed with shovels. They learned the storm had caused not one but 17 avalanches above a 3.5-km stretch of road. It was reported that over 2,600 people were trapped in their vehicles beneath several metres of snow as well as inside the tunnel. Some vehicles had been swept off the road and down the mountain on the other side.

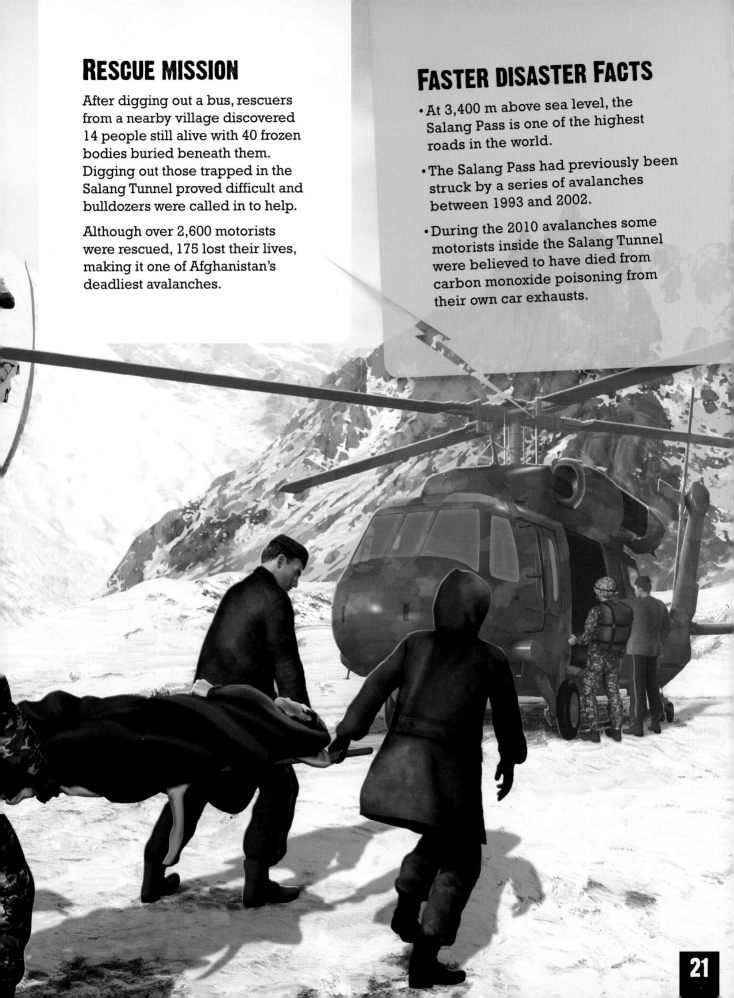

RESCUE MISSION

After digging out a bus, rescuers from a nearby village discovered 14 people still alive with 40 frozen bodies buried beneath them. Digging out those trapped in the Salang Tunnel proved difficult and bulldozers were called in to help.

Although over 2,600 motorists were rescued, 175 lost their lives, making it one of Afghanistan's deadliest avalanches.

FASTER DISASTER FACTS

- At 3,400 m above sea level, the Salang Pass is one of the highest roads in the world.

- The Salang Pass had previously been struck by a series of avalanches between 1993 and 2002.

- During the 2010 avalanches some motorists inside the Salang Tunnel were believed to have died from carbon monoxide poisoning from their own car exhausts.

WHAT'S IN AN AVALANCHE?

An avalanche is a mass of unstable ice and snow that suddenly slides down a mountainside. Avalanches can reach speeds of up to 320 kph and contain enough force to sweep away people, knock over trees and bury buildings. An avalanche can happen almost anywhere there is snow, a slope and a trigger to set it off.

ANATOMY OF AN AVALANCHE

An avalanche is made up of three main parts. The **starting zone** is the section at the top of a mountain slope where the snow is most unstable. An avalanche begins when this snow breaks loose and begins to slide.

As the snow picks up speed, it collects more snow, ice and rock and travels down a path known as the **track**. This is usually free of obstacles such as trees.

The snow finally comes to a stop and piles up in the bottom region, called the **runout zone**.

STARTING ZONE

TRACK

RUNOUT ZONE

| Weakest |
| Weak |
| Strong |
| Weakest |
| Ice |
| Strong |
| Weak |
| Weakest |
| Ground |

SNOWPACKS

Layers of snow are called snowpacks. Each layer contains a different kind of snow that has been formed by a particular type of weather.

Avalanche-prone snowpacks have layers of thin, weak snow, positioned between thicker layers of hard snow. This makes the whole snowpack unstable enough to cause an avalanche.

WHAT CAUSES AN AVALANCHE?

Avalanches are usually triggered by wind, rain, heavy snowfall, earthquakes, volcanoes, a rise in temperature or human activity. The weight of someone skiing or walking can set off an avalanche, as can a snowmobile.

AVALANCHE TYPES

To the untrained eye all avalanches look alike. However, there are two main types of avalanche: powder and slab. These types behave with different degrees of speed and power. Both are potentially deadly to humans unlucky enough to be caught by them.

POWDER AVALANCHE

Powdered snow is formed during very cold, dry weather. It is made up of snowflakes that do not bond together well, creating unstable snow. If this snow lies on a hard, icy layer of snow, then it becomes even more unstable.

Strong winds or new, heavy snowfalls can trigger avalanches of powered snow. As the snow travels downwards at speeds that can reach 320 kph, it can accumulate to create snowballs.

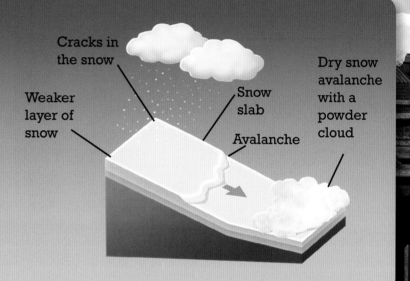

Cracks in the snow

Weaker layer of snow

Snow slab

Avalanche

Dry snow avalanche with a powder cloud

SLAB AVALANCHE

A slab avalanche starts off as a frozen layer of weak snow. When new heavy snowfall lands on top of this layer, it forms another layer known as a slab. If a trigger, such as a skier or snowmobile travels, over this snow, they can break the weak layer below and cause the slab on top to slide downwards.

A slab avalanche can reach speeds of up to 130 kph within five seconds. As it descends downwards, the slab often breaks up into smaller chunks, which are capable of destroying whole villages.

Crown

Left flank

Bed surface

Stauch wall

Right flank

WET AVALANCHES

Wet avalanches occur when sunshine, warm air or rain changes the chemical makeup of a snowpack and saturates it with water. This can create a slow-moving avalanche that seldom travels faster than 40 kph. However, wet avalanches can be dense and heavy enough to cause great destruction.

PEOPLE AND AVALANCHES

Avalanches are unpredictable and difficult to monitor. Many happen in remote mountainous regions. However, in more built-up areas, scientists research avalanche-prone areas. This helps people avoid likely spots where an avalanche might happen.

AVALANCHE WARNINGS

Several countries have avalanche organisations which work to predict and prevent avalanches. To do this, scientists collect snow samples from mountainsides and study their different layers. The scientists then combine their findings with weather reports and release avalanche warnings in particular areas. The avalanche danger is given a rating between 1 (low) and 5 (extreme).

NORTH AMERICAN PUBLIC AVALANCHE DANGER SCALE

Avalanche danger is determined by the likelihood, size and distribution of avalanches.

Danger Level		Travel Advice
EXTREME		Avoid all areas where an avalanche could occur.
HIGH		Very dangerous avalanche conditions. Do not travel in avalanche-prone areas.
CONSIDERABLE		Dangerous avalanche conditions. Check snowpacks. Choose routes carefully and be cautious of avalanche-prone areas.
MODERATE		Avalanche conditions are more likely in avalanche-prone areas. Check snowpacks. Identify routes and slopes where avalanches could occur.
LOW		Generally safe avalanche conditions. Watch out for unstable snow on isolated slopes and in avalanche-prone areas.
NO RATING		Watch out for and avoid slopes with recent avalanches or unstable snow. Signs are cracking in the snow or the sound of snowpacks collapsing.

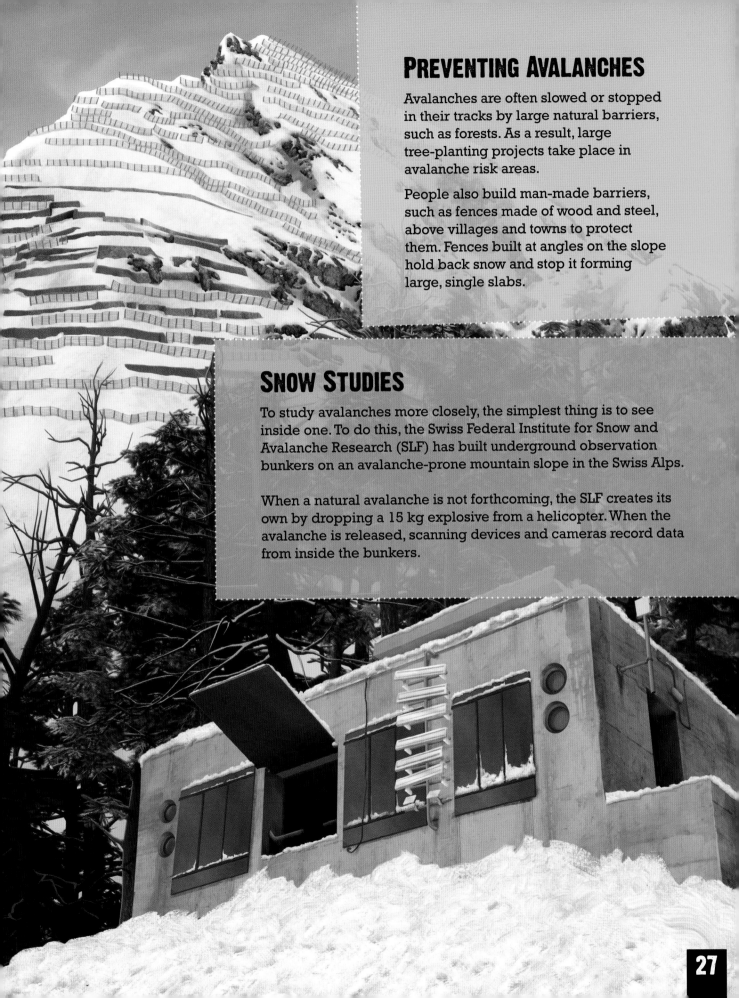

PREVENTING AVALANCHES

Avalanches are often slowed or stopped in their tracks by large natural barriers, such as forests. As a result, large tree-planting projects take place in avalanche risk areas.

People also build man-made barriers, such as fences made of wood and steel, above villages and towns to protect them. Fences built at angles on the slope hold back snow and stop it forming large, single slabs.

SNOW STUDIES

To study avalanches more closely, the simplest thing is to see inside one. To do this, the Swiss Federal Institute for Snow and Avalanche Research (SLF) has built underground observation bunkers on an avalanche-prone mountain slope in the Swiss Alps.

When a natural avalanche is not forthcoming, the SLF creates its own by dropping a 15 kg explosive from a helicopter. When the avalanche is released, scanning devices and cameras record data from inside the bunkers.

CASE STUDY: HUASCARAN, 1970

On 31 May 1970, the deadliest avalanche in modern history struck Peru. The avalanche was triggered by a powerful earthquake, which flattened dozens of Peruvian towns and villages. The quake also broke a vast section of glacial ice and rock free from a large volcano called Mount Huascaran. This caused the massive 'Nevados Huascaran' avalanche to crash down the mountainside.

DEVASTATION

The avalanche travelled for 18 km as it thundered down Mount Huascaran. Ice mixed with rock and mud, as the avalanche reached speeds of 335 kph. The towns of Yungay and Ranrahirca, which sat at the bottom of Mount Huascaran, were completely buried beneath over 50 m of avalanche debris. Only 400 of Yungay's population of 18,500 survived. In Ranrahirca, 2,000 were killed.

RESCUE

It took over two days for rescue teams to reach the buried towns of Yungay and Ranrahirca. In the meantime, survivors had been searching for loved ones by digging out rubble with their bare hands. But instead of trying to dig out all of the dead bodies, the Peruvian government declared the site a mass grave. All future excavation at the site has been forbidden.

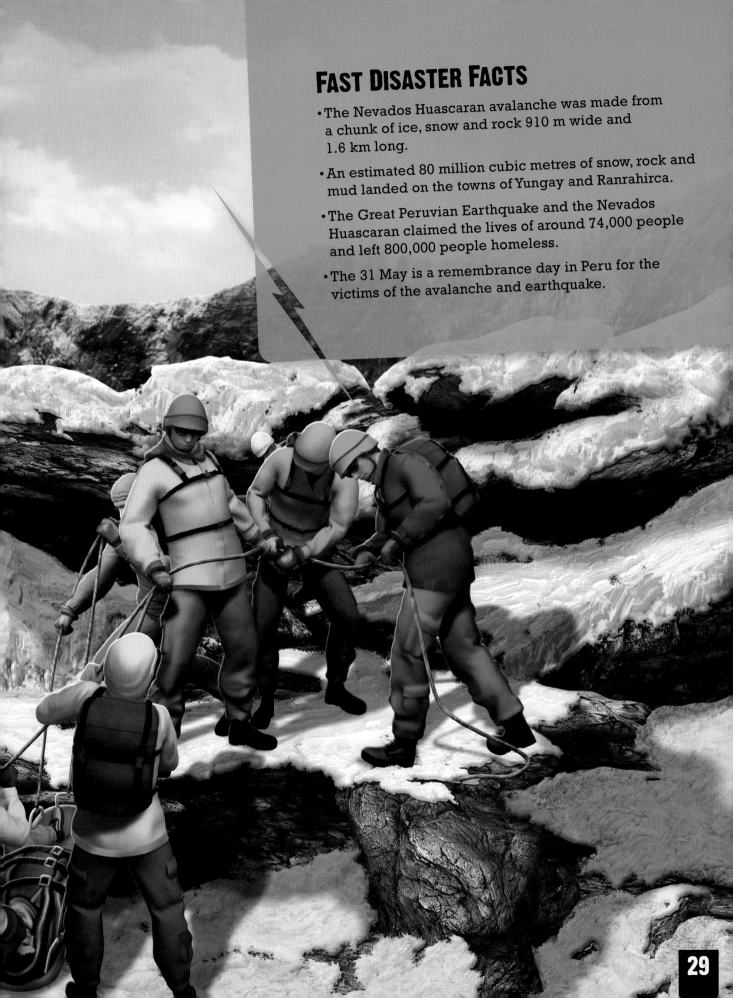

FAST DISASTER FACTS

- The Nevados Huascaran avalanche was made from a chunk of ice, snow and rock 910 m wide and 1.6 km long.

- An estimated 80 million cubic metres of snow, rock and mud landed on the towns of Yungay and Ranrahirca.

- The Great Peruvian Earthquake and the Nevados Huascaran claimed the lives of around 74,000 people and left 800,000 people homeless.

- The 31 May is a remembrance day in Peru for the victims of the avalanche and earthquake.

GLOSSARY, BOOKS AND HELPFUL WEBSITES

GLOSSARY

acid rain
Polluted rainfall that causes harm to the environment it falls on

archipelago
A groupe of islands

atmosphere
The gases surrounding the earth

atomic bomb
A bomb that creates a violent explosion through the release of nuclear energy

carbon monoxide
A colourless, odourless gas that is toxic to humans

continents
Seven massive areas of land that make up the Earth's land

debris
Pieces of rubbish and the remains of buildings which are scattered everywhere

displaced
Force someone to leave their home because of a natural disaster

Earth's crust
The layer closest to the surface of our planet

evacuation
The orderly removal of people from a place to avoid a disaster

exclusion zone
An area where it is forbidden for people to go

extinct
No longer alive or in existence

famine
A great lack of food over a wide area

geyser
A hot spring which sends a column of hot water and steam into the air

glacier
A slow-moving mass of ice formed on mountainsides

incinerate
Destroy something by burning it

magma
Molten rock flowing beneath the Earth

mantle
A layer of the Earth that makes up 85 per cent of the entire planet. The mantle is mostly solid rock but some parts are hotter and more fluid

mantle plume
A column of hot rock that rises through the Earth's mantle

observatory
A building dedicated to studying the stars or natural phenomena on Earth, such as volcanoes

ocean basin
A large dip of the earth's surface in which an ocean lies

pumice
A very light volcanic rock made from bubbly lava

satellite
An object that orbits a star or planet. Many Earth satellites are man-made objects that can take photos and record data about the planet

tectonic plate
A section of Earth's crust

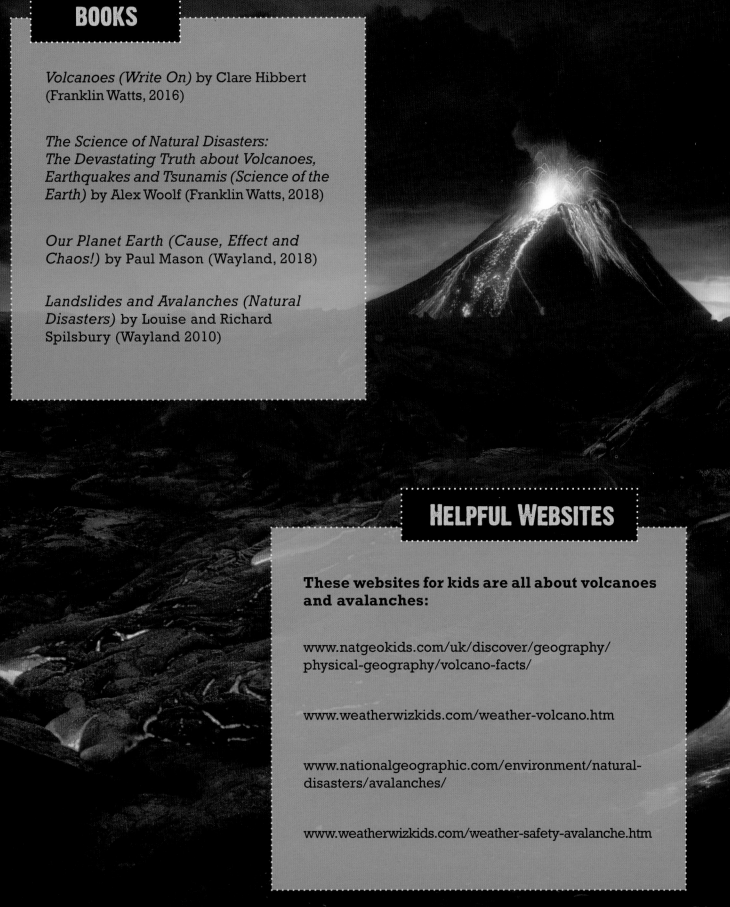

BOOKS

Volcanoes (Write On) by Clare Hibbert (Franklin Watts, 2016)

The Science of Natural Disasters: The Devastating Truth about Volcanoes, Earthquakes and Tsunamis (Science of the Earth) by Alex Woolf (Franklin Watts, 2018)

Our Planet Earth (Cause, Effect and Chaos!) by Paul Mason (Wayland, 2018)

Landslides and Avalanches (Natural Disasters) by Louise and Richard Spilsbury (Wayland 2010)

HELPFUL WEBSITES

These websites for kids are all about volcanoes and avalanches:

www.natgeokids.com/uk/discover/geography/physical-geography/volcano-facts/

www.weatherwizkids.com/weather-volcano.htm

www.nationalgeographic.com/environment/natural-disasters/avalanches/

www.weatherwizkids.com/weather-safety-avalanche.htm

INDEX

Afghanistan 20–21
archaeologists 15
ash 4, 6, 8–12, 14, 17
avalanches 4, 20–29
  how avalanches form 22–23
powder 24
preventing 27
slab 24
types of avalanche 24–25
  wet 25
  zones (starting/runout) 22

bombs 12

caldera 16–17
cones 9
crust, Earth's 8–9

earthquakes 6, 17–19, 23,
  28–29

fireballs 6, 9

gases 4, 6–10, 12–14, 17–19
geysers 16
Great Peruvian Earthquake
  28–29

Hawaii 9
Herculaneum 14–15

Indonesia 6–7
Italy 14–15

lahars 13
lava 4, 6, 8–12, 16, 18–19
  aa 12
  pahoehoe 12

magma 8–11, 16
mantle, Earth's 8–9, 16
Mauna Loa 9
Mount Huascaran 28–29
Mount Merapi, Java 6–7
Mount Vesuvius 14–15, 19

Nevado del Ruiz 13
Nevados Huascaran
  avalanche 28–29
North American Public
  Avalanche Danger Scale 26

observatories, volcano 19

Peru 28–29
plates, tectonic 8–9
plumes, mantle 9
Pompeii 14–15
pumice 14
pyroclastic flows 6, 12–14

Ring of Fire 5, 7
Rome, ancient 14–15

Salang Pass, Afghanistan
  20–21
seismometers 19

snow 4–5, 20–29
snowpacks 23, 25–26
snowstorms 5
spots, hot 9, 16
supervolcanoes 16–17
Swiss Federal Institute for
  Snow and Avalanche
  Research 27

track, avalanche 22

USA 16–17

vents 8–11, 18
Vesuvius Observatory 19
volcanoes 4–19, 23, 28
  cinder cone 11
classification 11
composite 10
how volcanoes form 8–9
  lava dome 11
shield 10
  stratovolcanoes 10
types of volcano 10–11
volcanologists 15, 17–19

warnings, avalanche 26–27

Yellowstone National Park
  16–17

NATURAL DISASTER Z⚡NE

SERIES CONTENT LIST

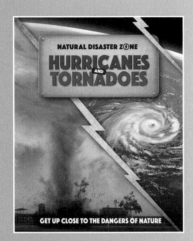

Introducing tornadoes and hurricanes • When a tornado strikes • What's in a tornado? • Tornado winds • Case study: Moore, 2013 • Studying tornadoes • Storm chasers • When a hurricane hits • What makes hurricanes form? • What's in a hurricane? • Categories ofhurricane • Case study: mitch, 1998 • Studying hurricanes • Glossary, books and helpful websites • Index

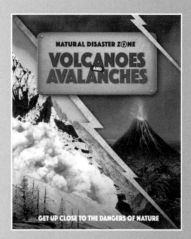

Introducing volcanoes and avalanches • When a volcano erupts • What's in a volcano? • Types of volcanoes • Rock, gas, ash and lava • Case study: Vesuvius, ce 79 • Super volcanoes • People and volcanoes • When an avalanche is released • What's in an avalanche? • Avalanche types • People and avalanches • Case study: Huascaran, 1970 • Glossary, books and helpful websites • Index

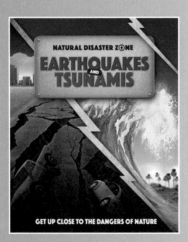

When an earthquake strikes • A word of plates • What's in an earthquake? • Seismic shockwaves • Case study: Kathmandu, 2015 • Predicting earthquakes • When a tsunami strikes • What's in a tsunami? • Case study: Japan, 2011 • Emergency crews • Predicting tsunamis • Preparing for tsunamis • Glossary, books and helpful websites • Index

Introducing wildfires and freak weather • When a wildfire ignites • Types of wildfire • Parts of a wildfire • Case study: Victoria, 2009 • Wildfire fighters • Preventing fire • Freak weather • Heatwaves and drought • Flash floods • Ice storms • Dust storms • Fish rain and orange snow • Glossary, books and helpful websites • Index